SURFING LIFE WAVES

Surfing Life Waves

by **Bradley Hook**

photography by

Jules Phillips

& Rhydian Thomas

A Dispersion Publishing Book

www.dispersion.co

dispersion
publishing

Cover photo © Jules Phillips (www.oceaneye.com.au)
Previous and current page photos © Rhydian Thomas
(www.bayflare.com)

Hook, Bradley

Surfing Life Waves / by Bradley Hook

ISBN 978-0-9874628-0-0

www.surfinglifewaves.com

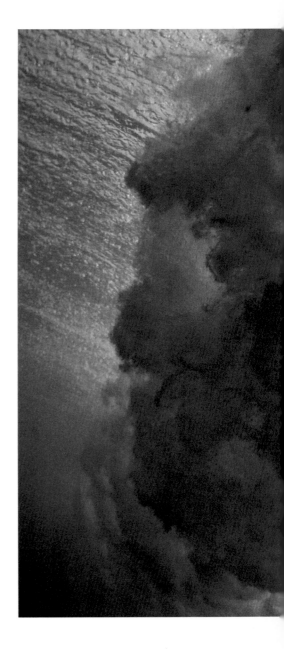

Dedicated to the ocean

who gives us everything

CONTENTS

"Surfing teaches me acceptance,
patience and balance.

From the ocean, from surfing, I feel like
I get feedback and I know whether I'm
on the right course or not.

I'm able to get all of life's lessons
from it."

Kelly Slater

INTRODUCTION

Waves are all around us. Light waves, sound waves, radio waves, electromagnetic waves, microwaves, seismic waves, gamma waves, elusive gravitational waves and scientific quantum waves. We describe waves of relief, success, anxiety and sadness; heat waves, shock waves and brain waves. Your heartbeat itself is a series of waves reflecting your innermost energy, your life force, and can be easily seen on an ECG machine at your local hospital. Waves are the constant that underpin our reality – perhaps the unifying element and source of all life. Even the recently detected Higgs boson – sometimes called the "God particle" – is a ripple in a wave field that may unveil our universe's greatest secrets.

With all this wave activity it's easy to compare the scientific and metaphorical waves we know so well to the more abstract experiential waves we are faced with in life. Opportunities for success, failure, love and a spectrum of enriching experiences come to us in the form of waves every day. Every opportunity is energy pulsing in synchronicity towards you. Using the approach of the surfer, arguably the world's foremost experts in waves, you can embrace the opportunities that colour your existence with exuberance, awareness and a lot less attachment to the outcome.

Surfing Life Waves is as much a guide for the author who transcribed it as it may become for anyone who happens to identify with and enjoy the following pages. Using this approach you'll discover how the more you practice catching waves of opportunity, the better you'll get at riding them. You'll find that you can't control waves: they will break where they will break. What you can control is that you are geographically, physically and mentally in the best possible position to make the most of the waves that do crash into your life. It's a path destined to throw you into the depths more than if you stayed safely on the beach. But a life spent on the beach, watching others, is not the life of a surfer.

You may have already ridden or missed the best waves of your life, or maybe the perfect waves of your dreams are brewing in a storm far away. It doesn't matter, don't be attached to what you can't control. Focus on what you came here to do, which is to go surfing.

"Matter is a wave of potential."

Deepak Chopra

SURF CHECK

Sometimes it's a dash to the end of the street and sometimes a voyage across continents. Deciding when and where to surf is integral to every surfing experience. The surf check can be as hands-on as driving to the beach at dawn or as detached as scanning a long-range forecast on the internet. Using a combination of knowledge, intuition, technology and luck, surfers tirelessly seek the location – and waves – that will provide an optimal surfing experience.

When you feel a longing for new challenges or yearn for something more from life, it's time to go and find a place where those waves of opportunity are breaking.

As humans we are consciously and unconsciously always seeking pleasure and avoiding pain – it's the most basic element of our nature. This worked well for hunter-gatherers but in the industrialised world where death and scarcity are often not direct concerns, results in a lot of aimlessness, dissatisfaction and regret. Understanding what we are searching for is one part of life's journey and understanding why is another. Finding clarity through having a vision helps bridge the two. Surfers conjure up images of their perfect waves with fetish-like detail. The cylindrical shape, colour, dimensions, lightly-feathered peeling lip.

Take some time to consider the waves of opportunity you dream of riding in your life. When you can visualise them your search can begin. In the future you may discover how, at a certain point, you no longer need goals because life becomes a goal unto itself – but, for now, a vision is a good place to start. This vision – and understanding of what you really want – imbues a sense of purpose and direction, which gives life meaning.

And the meaning of life is... whatever you want it to be.

There is an ocean of opportunities constantly swirling around you. Some are small and seemingly insignificant, a rare few are perfect and many are daunting or downright terrifying. Sometimes you may feel you're experiencing a lull – no job, no dates, seemingly no prospects – when at other times you have too many options. This is all part of nature's interminable rhythm.

The essence of the surf check is that you get yourself out there and look around. Stop. Breathe. Use your intuition, your knowledge and technology. Remember to distinguish between what you want and need. They are very different things, so invest your energy wisely. Material desires are fine but objects rarely fill the spaces in your heart.

Living with passion, finding love and experiencing flow will.

Search regularly and be open to opportunities that might not look as good as you'd hoped. Waves are much more fun when you're in the water than while you sit on the beach deliberating. Be persistent in your search because there will be special days when the wind is still or offshore and the ocean turns silky... when the wave energy begins to pulse towards your little stretch of land. And when the elements align with your desires and willing presence you will find dream waves

to provide you with life's most exhilarating and fulfilling experiences. Perfect waves are always breaking somewhere and the perfect wave is different for everyone. Getting plenty of practice means you'll be prepared when your dream waves come along.

The best surfers are often the most intrepid. Guys and girls who are prepared to venture beyond their local break are usually the same ones who surf best when they are back at home. Exposing yourself to a range of opportunities gives your life depth. If you always check the surf at the same place you'll get pretty good at riding those waves but life is extreme and there is so much beauty, danger and richness out there to be explored. That's not to say you shouldn't just surf at home if it makes you happy.

Right now you may be waiting for the perfect opportunity – to meet "the one", to land the dream job, to get healthy... but if you're not at the right beach you'll never get the chance.

Einstein said that insanity is doing the same thing over and over, hoping for a different result. He is, of course, right (and, incidentally, had a fascination with waves).

Sometimes as surfers we venture far from our local beach only to end up back at home several tedious hours later... just as the wind changes direction, rendering the surf a mess. There is always the risk of falling into the grass is greener – "waves might be better just over the next headland" trap. If it looks good sometimes you just have to get out there. Don't over-think the situation. You meet a girl: she's funny, cute and lives next door. Are you really going to forsake asking her on a date because you may meet a supermodel later tonight? Don't over-think.

But also be prepared to get fit, learn a new language and fly to Hawaii so you do get a shot with the supermodel. If you don't someone else certainly will.

If you're not finding the right waves maybe you need a geographic change, to get out of a dead-end relationship or to leave a stagnant job. Maybe you just need to re-evaluate what you really want and need. You may already be riding your dream life waves.

The surf check is where you get excited about life. Use your intuition, assess the conditions and go searching.

PREPARATION

When the waves are good surfers usually jump right in, but a little preparation can exponentially enhance your wave-riding experience. When you watch professional surfers, who ride waves because their livelihood depends on it, you'll notice intricate detail in their pre-surf preparation. Some sit in meditative silence, some listen to music to get 'psyched', some run through complex warm-up and stretch routines.

Before harnessing the waves of opportunity that spill into your life there are things you can do. Some are obvious. Being healthy not only extends your life but enriches your experience of it. When your body is functioning optimally you free your mind to be completely engaged in the conscious experience. You are more fearless, brash and you will be more likely to push yourself into situations beyond your perceived realms of comfort. It is beyond your comfort zone that the magic happens.

When you're feeling good you will make decisions with clarity, you'll embrace positive change boldly and rebound from failure quickly. You will lead a more courageous and graceful life when you are feeling well.

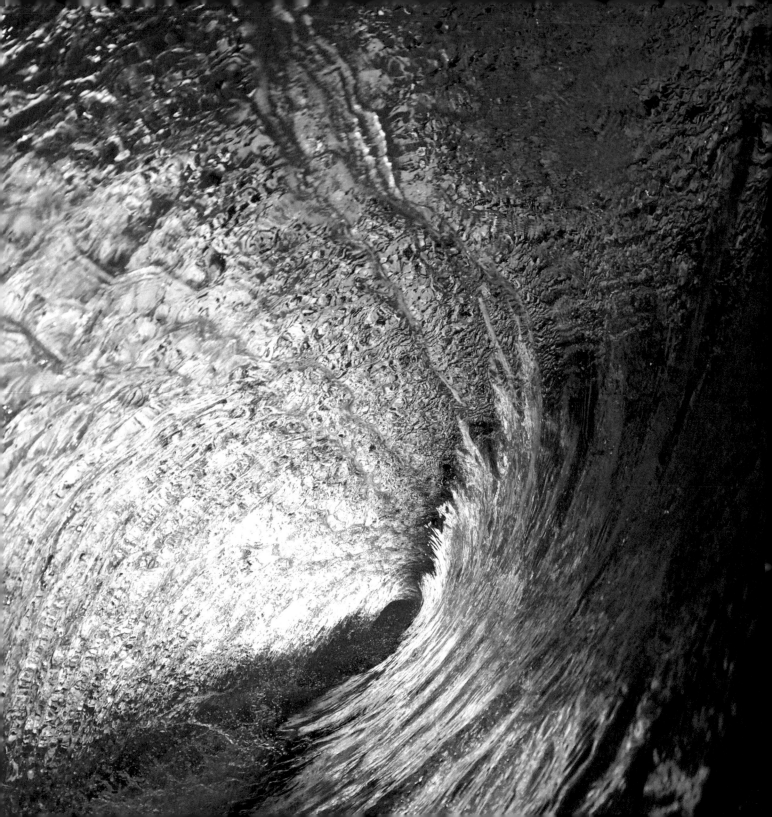

Visualisation can be as powerful as doing and provides a method for embedding a goal more deeply into your subconscious. In studies, people who visualised an exercise gained the same muscle mass as those actually doing it (granted, they visualised vividly and with great effort).

Simulating situations mentally before they occur gives you a sense of confidence – you've been there, it's not as scary. Surfers can't help but imagine catching the waves of their dreams. There's hardly a surfer for whom the right-shaped tree doesn't become a gaping barrel or a steep slope a perfect wave. We're always visualising our dream waves as well as watching other surfers catch them out in the water and in surf movies.

In life you can do the same. Visualise your interactions with others, especially those that will progress you towards your dreams. Do it positively, do it meditatively, do it with a smile. Even the interactions you dread usually turn out better than expected. Visualise what it will look and feel like to be riding that wave of happiness that you seek, be it in a relationship, career, attaining freedom, whatever. You don't have to rehearse affirmations, mantras or behest the Universe's participation.

Just use your imagination, that's what it's for.

Finally, always keep visualisation and expectation separate. Don't think you deserve your dream waves, for neither nature nor life can be controlled. Existence is a drunkard's walk where so much of what happens occurs due to chance or being at the right place at the right time. What you can control is that when your chances come along you're as prepared as you can possibly be.

You'll never regret the time and effort spent developing yourself to be your best.

THE PADDLE

O ften overlooked or considered a hindrance, the paddle-out provides a highly targeted warm-up whether surfers like it or not. It's easy to dread, especially at beach breaks where the waves peak and spill towards the shore haphazardly, eager to keep land creatures terranean.

The paddle in life is tackling the small steps required to achieve a goal. You can procrastinate and avoid the annoying, tedious and difficult

tasks or you can embrace them with exuberance. The sooner you get them done, the sooner you get to surf.

After plunging into the ocean you can quickly begin to feel insignificant. Earth's saline lifeblood has no favourites. It is with a combination of luck, timing and your own personal strength that you will find your way out to where the waves – the opportunities – are. Surfers learn to duck dive, to paddle wide away from the breaking waves and to avoid obstructing other surfers who are already riding waves, even if it means taking a beating themselves.

Getting to the place where the waves of opportunity are takes persistence. If your goal is to be healthy there are a series of steps between you right now and the glowing you of the future. These steps are the paddle. There will be obstacles and there will be difficulties but the more you paddle the stronger you'll get. Don't think too much about the waves breaking out there, keep your attention on your immediate surroundings and stay focused.

As you gain momentum look up occasionally to make sure you're on track. If you are working towards launching a new business you may find yourself overwhelmed by the sheer volume of distractions, obstacles and difficulties encumbering your progress. Don't despair. Remember that every obstacle was once someone else's opportunity. Obstacles and opportunities are all water in the same ocean, it just depends from where you're looking.

Never ruin someone else's opportunity. Even if it means taking a beating and getting spun like a rag-doll in the depths, cheer your friend or a stranger on as he catches the wave of his life. Happiness is best shared, so be encouraging and never obstruct anyone else's dream – even if you think you know what's best. You will have your turn so keep your head down and get out to where your wave is waiting.

Don't resent the paddle. It will warm you up, it will test your courage, it will make the waves you ride even sweeter. When you're working towards a dream embrace the obstacles – they're as much part of the dream as the elation when you achieve it. Otherwise what kind of dreams do you have, if they are so easy to achieve? Become one with your goal and you'll find there is no good or bad, it's just how you perceive the experience.

It takes practice not to dislike waves that push us backwards and toss us like the insignificant beings we are. But waves are just waves: energy in motion, even the experiential ones that impede or delight us in life. No wave lasts forever. When you're in an underwater tempest being thrashed so hard that you don't know which way is up – relax. Conserve your energy. The most successful people have invariably taken the most beatings. It's just an experience, it is not you. Smile with courage and defiance you'll be filled with new vigour. Be strong and resilient and never give up.

Even if you get washed to the beach without catching a wave it's ok. Just make sure you come back tomorrow and try again.

"The journey is the thing."

Homer

The Line-Up

You've made it out beyond the breakers, to where the ocean is ominous and electric. This is where the waves live. You're ready and now all you have to do is... negotiate the crowd, evaluate the ever-changing elements and find the right position – all whilst maintaining complete awareness of where the pulsing energy of nature's liquid heart will peak up and spill as your wave.

In an increasingly crowded world it's not surprising that even surfing's aloha spirit has given way to incidents of surf anger and even full-blown rage. Our world has limited space, limited resources and limited waves of opportunity at any one time. Greed doesn't work, it creates anger, violence, hatred – ugliness. Many are the stories of a greedy man brought back to earth both literally and metaphorically. The key is to become the best surfer you can be, so you get your rightful share of waves. Being intrepid and creative can go a long way towards finding you waves in places where others might not be looking. Being bold will get you onto the biggest waves that most people are too afraid to catch.

In life you've put yourself out there, you've decided that you want something and you've done the hard work to get you to the brink. It may be the job interview, it may be eye contact with the stranger, it may be saving up for your big investment. There are others wanting what you want, or perhaps the opportunity is fleeting, so how will you make sure you catch this wave?

Position yourself right. Before you paddled out you may have seen where the best waves were breaking, or where those wide ones broke when the sets rolled in. Find yourself a landmark, stick to it and don't get dragged away by the current. You've set yourself a goal and you've invested a lot of energy – don't lose sight of why you're out there. It's too easy to get swept away in life's minutiae. Keep focused and maintain your position, even if you have to paddle hard to stay there. Remember, everyone else is struggling too. If it is too crowded or you're not strong enough perhaps you're surfing in the wrong place. Geography can simply transform your life. There are far more opportunities for waves in remote places – but you have to weigh up what you'll miss about home.

Sometimes you have to be realistic and adaptable. Instead of competing against the crowd with a low chance of getting an opportunity, you'll find freedom and peace sitting far to the side, waiting for those rogue ones that everyone else will miss.

You can also be friendly and flash a smile or say hello. In life, as in surfing, networking gets you places. Being positive and enthusiastic helps in a hypersocial world.

Some surfers hang on the shoulder of every wave hoping the person up and riding will fail, so they can grab it. People will always be hoping for you to fail. Don't worry about it, you have enough going on – stop thinking and focus on your wave!

Sometimes there is no escaping the crowds and you just have to get involved. You'll think some people have all the luck, seemingly in the right place every time. The more you practice the luckier you'll get. When the wave you've been waiting for comes along and you're in prime position, paddle with all the determination you have. People notice and they will pull back and let you go. If they don't you're probably surfing in the wrong place.

Be strategic and find a balance between being assertive, timid and greedy.

THE WAVE

Waves are borne of energy from the sun. Through wind convection and a million other variables a pulse of water is projected towards a land mass, literally ripples in a big blue pond on our precious home, Earth. When this swell arrives, if the force against the ocean's floor is great enough, it will steepen and spill forth as a wave, no two ever the same. In life, waves of opportunity are everywhere. Identifying the right ones and learning to ride them takes practice, dedication and hard work. When you've identified the right wave for you – whether it's a new relationship, career, adventure or goal – and the opportunity arrives, do everything you can to catch it. Paddle with determination, commitment, focus and instinct. This is where you synchronise yourself with the opportunity.

The ghosts of people you didn't become linger always around you. When you get an opportunity, even a small one, treat it as sacred. Sometimes waves that seem irrelevant can give you the perfect experience, partly because it was unexpected. Often all it takes is a change of board, or attitude, to appreciate what has been there all along.

Your wave is here, you're looking into the abyss (and the abyss is looking into you) so gather momentum and, in the words of every surf instructor anywhere, "paddle, paddle, paddle!"

THE DROP

Exhilarating, weightless, momentary, profound... the drop is all about commitment. You've harnessed a new opportunity and now there is no turning back. This is where you let yourself go, be electric, find your feet and embrace the rush of new experience. You may fail, but you will learn. If you do not fail, all you can do is succeed. Pulling back now almost always ends in those spectacular time-suspending, over-the-falls wipe-outs other surfers love to watch.

There are many types of drops. If you have paddled fast enough you will probably get to your feet with plenty of time to scope out the oncoming wave. If you've rushed into a late drop you'll undoubtedly be on your toes, quite literally, as you free fall into what could be the ride of your life.

The drop is where you get your initial momentum, so don't hold back. In life you may surprise even yourself by jumping into waves of opportunity that sneak up on you. This is reality: people make decisions with implications that change their lives in moments of love, hate, lust or irrational rage. Everything from saying hello to the cute stranger to saving someone's life, from affairs to impulse purchases... late drops –

jumping into things – shake you out of complacency. They can be good or bad but we need them, because taking risks makes us feel alive.

It's generally advised that the types of opportunities you take in moments of madness are within your skill and experience level to manage, or at least comprehend. Alcohol severely enhances the appearance of some opportunities in life, often with rather disappointing consequences (but a good tale to tell). Never stop learning and remember the greatest risks yield the greatest rewards. If you're following your heart you can never go wrong, even in failure.

The drop can be the most exhilarating part of the surfing experience. Big wave surfers live for it. The opportunity is before you – you've said hello to the beautiful stranger, you've accepted the job, you're about to sign that dotted line – don't pull back. Don't even think of pulling back. Don't even think. Life is about moments of heightened emotion whether good or bad. This is your heightened moment, relish and embrace it. This is you – alive.

THE BOTTOM TURN

Every proficient surfer will agree that the first bottom turn sets the tone for an entire wave. It's a fluid swooping motion whereby surfers convert the speed of gravity and the wave's momentum into their own line upon a transient watery canvas.

You've taken the drop, made it and now the wall of potential is rushing forth to meet you. This is where you propel yourself onto a trajectory that determines the speed and power of that first critical manoeuvre. Unless you're doomed to failure – and you'll know when you are – don't give up. Wherever you look is where you will go. Glance down at reef below you and chances are you'll be meeting some sea urchins fairly soon; look out to the wall of the wave and that is where you'll race to safety. Good surfers focus upwards to the power pocket, the critical slope where the wave spills energy back towards itself, which is the most exciting and dangerous of surfing realms.

In life the bottom turn is your intention. It's the way in which you're about to harness this wave of opportunity. You can aim for high performance and put everything you have on the line or you can cruise lazily, observing the world around or within you. Some surfers exude a timeless grace in the bottom turn and the same can be achieved in life.

At this pivotal moment you get an idea of what is possible. You've gone for that new job and landed it. Will you strive for high performance and risk failing? Or glide easily towards the shoulder with no real objective? There is no right or wrong. The key is to set an intention and stick to it. If you want to fly then look up towards the steepest section and propel yourself there with speed and power.

If you're learning you'll want to take it slow to avoid ruining an entire wave of opportunity by falling too soon. You can try asking for a pay rise in your first week or running a marathon after a day of training – but you may fail, probably spectacularly so.

Once you've grasped a new opportunity in your life you can decide where you wish to take it. Not every wave needs to be annihilated, sometimes cruising can be just as fulfilling and fun.

This is where you get to decide.

THE RIDE

You've picked your line and now you're a living being literally harnessing a wave of moving energy. Andy Irons said that the act of surfing is like being kissed by God. He is right. Once you've ridden a good wave you can't help but want to experience the rush again and again. Imagine if you could live your life with this enthusiasm and joy. It is possible.

The secret is… that there is no secret. In life – as in surfing – you ride your waves of opportunity in ways that reflect your personality, mood, skills and objectives. For a fulfilled, if not blissful, life you just have to find yourself spending more time flowing with the kinds of opportunities that you love.

Flow – as defined in the field of positive psychology – is the state of being completely immersed in an activity you love, to the point where time seemingly stands still. It is the ultimate experience where you literally become your actions and your actions become you. To reach flow with the waves of opportunity that crash into your life you need practice doing whatever it is you love. It is said that mastery of an activity takes 10,000 hours and this is fine because you have been catching waves of opportunity since birth. To be reading this book

confirms you are already a master of sorts. But if your goal is to be Prime Minister then you need some serious practice on some pretty heavy political waves. Nothing beats time spent in the water so once you have a vision, ride as many waves as you can. In time you'll discover the energy and captivation of flow.

As pleasure-seeking-animals we sometimes choose to ride the wrong waves over and over while letting the right ones go out of laziness, fear or bad judgement. If you're riding the wrong waves consistently and you're not enjoying surfing it's time to change your approach or try a different beach.

Regardless of your goals and level of experience you can make the most of your life waves right now through simply having the right attitude. The key is exuberance. Be light, be curious and be exuberant. You are on a wave of opportunity: you've met the partner of your dreams or you've got that job. You've chosen a new field of study or volunteered for an organisation... be exuberant! Don't attach yourself to the outcome, just ride this opportunity for the sake of being part of it. And don't listen to those who may bring you down – the 'Dream Stealers' as Bear Grylls calls them. It really doesn't matter what anyone else thinks. Everyone who is alive today will be gone in a sprinkling of decades. Ride this wave with exuberance. If it offers a wall throw yourself up to the steep

part, the power pocket, and feel the elation as you drop back down with speed and power. Be creative and have fun. Gravity is the only thing that should ever bring you down. So defy it, embrace it and flow back to the power source – that place where the water peels back in on itself – and do it again. When you get good enough you may even begin to fly.

This is your life and you're surfing it.

"I could not help concluding this man had the most supreme pleasure while he was driven so fast and so smoothly by the sea."

Captain James Cooke

THE PADDLE BACK OUT

Different to the paddle at the start of your session, this is where you get to reflect on the wave you just rode. Sometimes the paddle back is effortless: you get swept out in a rip current or there's an easy channel back to the take-off zone, as found alongside most reef breaks. But often the paddle back out is a breathless struggle against pounding, relentless sets of oceanic fury. Either way, it's the perfect time for appreciating and processing the wave you just rode. This will often be a time for contemplating failure. Not for dwelling upon it for you'll soon be back in the line-up, open to fresh opportunities. But if ever there is a time to relive and recoil at your failures it is now. Replay the wave in your mind and learn from the experience. Paddle hard and aggressively if you need to let off steam and you'll get back out there with renewed resolve.

In life you sometimes get on a roll. Everything goes your way and you're in the right place at the right time without even trying. You've synchronised through luck, awareness and skill with the opportunities that are rising to meet you. Relish these times.

Sometimes you'll fight for an opportunity with all your might. You'll land that new job, you'll find that potential partner, you'll break that bad habit only to fail miserably at the critical moment. And when you come up for air you'll find the obstacles stacked up against you again. You can give up. Sure it's easy to go home and return to the comfort of old ways. Or you can give it another try. Don't be attached to the 'bad' experience that just transpired. You are not the experience, it was just a wave of energy that you rode. If someone hurt you in a relationship or you lost in a challenge or you failed in a work endeavour don't allow these experiences to define you. Learn from them, of course, but process and distinguish them as experiences.

The most successful people in life are not necessarily the most talented. Often they're just the most tenacious. Too much genius is lost through lack of perseverance and determination. Don't let this happen to you. Your only responsibility in life is to flower, to reach your full potential. You live once and you'll have plenty of rest when your ashes are scattered to a breeze. Get back out there, you'll rarely regret trying.

Remember, being mindful and reflective on the paddle back out will help you progress... unless you just scored the wave of your life in which case let your exhilaration shine through.

THE GLOW

You've caught your last wave of the day and your feet touch the sand. Maybe you just went through the "one last wave" syndrome, the bane of every gambler's life. Surfers sometimes find themselves caught in a cycle trying to get just one more – a good one – to finish the session. It's easy to end up feeling a little vulnerable as the sun dips, you're all alone and the ocean turns oily, dark and flat. It's good to know when you've had enough because there's nothing in surfing like finishing on a high.

After your session you're usually treated to a heady combination of exhilaration, exhaustion and – if the waves were good – stoke. Stoke is a blissful state of satisfaction, elated mindfulness: you've touched the essence of your being. All the worry in the world fades in a moment of stoke. Go down to your local beach on a day when the waves are clean and the winds offshore and you'll see it everywhere.

When you're out in the world pursuing whatever it is that you desire not every session will bring you happiness or enrichment. But you are always learning just by being out there – and every session makes you a better surfer. Even an average surf can provide a glow, for you've been out there, progressing, alive.

When you've had a great session you get to savour the experience and this is where you give gratitude for simply being alive. There will come a day when you can surf no more so bask in the aftermath of the moments that make you smile.

Life is not about the easy times, it is about the difficult ones, for those become the benchmark by which you judge everything else. So when you've caught a great wave – met the person of your dreams, been recognised for your talents, saved a life, planted a tree, said hello to the cute dog outside the supermarket – make sure you appreciate and be grateful for the experience. Give your mind a break, breathe in deeply, smile, feel complete.

THE TUBE

A philosophy taught by the ocean could never be complete without a special tribute to the tube. Those moments where you are sliding through the wave's heartspace, engulfed in the ocean's liquid embrace. It's the most revered aspect of the surfing experience and has disproportionate volumes of literature, art and film devoted to it. It is one of the riskiest places to be on a wave but also the most ethereal, fleeting and beautiful. The view from behind that curtain is as close to a religious experience as many of us will ever have.

In life, the tube is that moment when everything aligns. You're in perfect harmony with the opportunity, in the most critical and beautiful place. You've committed everything to this endeavour and now you're spiralling towards the light. You're boarding that plane, you're falling in love – if this goes well you'll never forget the moment. It's the greatest risk but only this will yield the greatest reward.

It's rare that you'll get barrelled accidentally. You know what you're getting into and you're usually jumping at the opportunity, if not actively seeking it out. Taking great risks while surfing the waves of your life takes years of practice to perfect. If you're dedicated and willing

to accept a lot of failure you'll become exceptional at riding the waves of your success, adventure and enrichment. You can be the one that everyone aspires to be, the person riding life's barrels fearlessly and with style.

CONCLUSION

You're surfing your way through life. The fear of failure is now a fear of not trying. When presented with waves of opportunity you balance risk with creativity and instinct. Sometimes you strive for progression: alive, exuberant. Sometimes you ride with style and grace. Other times you let someone else go and feel the glow of another person's stoke. Most of all you are embracing the waves as they come and riding them mindfully – with your full attention.

Don't wait for a catastrophe to shake you out of your sleep. Too many people function like robots on autopilot only to realise they need a change when it's almost too late. If you had all the money in the world what would you do? Now do it. Even just a little bit every day. You'll be surprised at where a bit of momentum can get you.

This is not a dress rehearsal for another, better life. Stop any self-loathing or negativity, it's a waste of precious energy. One day you'll look back with awe at the person you are today. Be open to new opportunities. Go out and search for the ones you feel you really need. Use your mind as a tool but your heart as a guide. Practice every day you can. Get fit and healthy. Smile unashamedly – life is too fleeting to worry about what anyone else thinks. When you get your life waves embrace them as magical, sacred experiences that illuminate your existence. But at the same time don't be attached to your experiences, good or bad. You are not the experience, you are a witness to what you do. Who is this witness? It's certainly not your noisy brain. It's that inexplicable part of you that loves being in the tube, being in flow.

When you become good enough at riding life waves you'll realise that you no longer need to set goals. You'll find that the right opportunities and experiences synchronise with you. It's a form of enlightenment: you become completely detached from the experience because you are intrinsically immersed in it. The experience becomes you and you become the experience. Your mind no longer fills your consciousness with noise, your heart overflows.

You've probably experienced moments like this in your life. Where you are so in tune, so in flow, so on form that you felt unstoppable, like a god. With practice, dedication and mindfulness you can ride your life waves like this always. You can become the whole ocean.

Embrace your life with exuberance and curiosity. Never stop surfing.

"You are part of an infinite energy,
a wave in an infinite ocean."

Osho

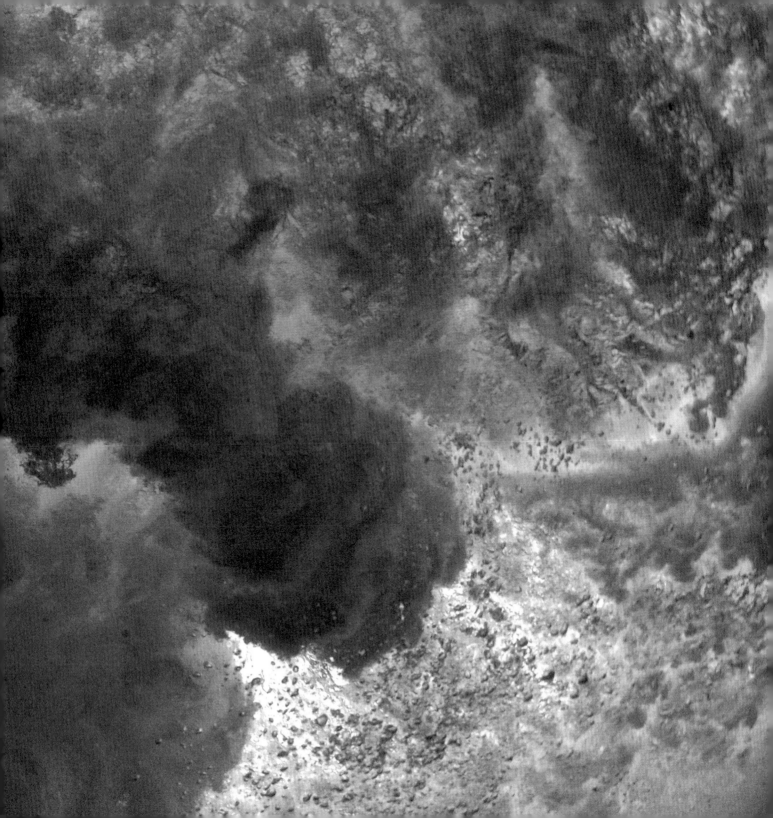

"I've always thought surfing
is a reflection of who you are."

Kelly Slater

PHOTOGRAPHY

Jules Phillips

As a kid I once stood on the summit of our highest mountain range and could barely make out the ocean on a clear day. The rural heartland of New Zealand's North Island is an amazing place to grow up but had I known what lay on the far horizon I might have taken my inflatable truck tyre all the way down the river at a much earlier age. The country life is awesome but it will now always be the waves and the ocean for me.

Either way, an appreciation for the outdoors gets well under your skin, just as the essence of surf culture builds and courses through your veins. Photography is just an extension of my own personal connection with my surroundings, like bush walking, bird watching or diving. Its hard not to become overwhelmed with astonishment by all the amazing things in the natural world and these are the things that keep me real, down to earth and grounded. If I can capture some of those magic moments forever as an image, then I am totally entertained and easy to please.

www.oceaneye.com.au

Rhydian Thomas

Rhydian is the owner of bayflare.com — a personal outlet of surf, ocean and coastal imagery, taken around the beaches of Sydney's eastern suburbs and from travels in Indonesia including West Sumbawa, Lombok and Bali. Originally from the south coast of Wales, having spent plenty of quality surf time in California, South Africa, NZ and Europe, Rhydian is now based in Bondi, Australia where he spends most of his time fixed behind the viewfinder.

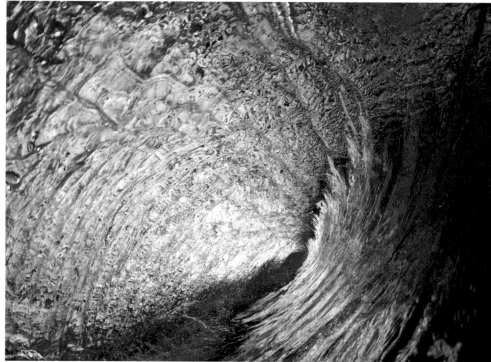

www.bayflare.com

Surfaid

SurfAid is a non-profit humanitarian organisation whose aim is to improve the health, wellbeing and self-reliance of people living in isolated regions connected to us through surfing.

Community development is about helping people to help themselves. It works by harnessing individual potential and transforming it through education and strong partnerships into just and sustainable solutions that build better futures for all. Huge possibility lies within each of each and every one of us, no matter how isolated our community might be, or how little formal education we may have received. The community development process is long and tricky. But given time, dedication and skills, it works and works well.

25 percent of the profits from the sale of this book will go to SurfAid.

www.surfaidinternational.org

CREDITS

Thank you to Kristen Gooding at Quiksilver for her help.

Thank you to Jules and Rhydian for contributing your inspiring, beautiful photography to this little book. Your images speak more than my words ever could.

Made in the USA
Middletown, DE
23 August 2018